Falling Into The Cracks

Alisha Redmond

Presentation by *BookLeaf Publishing*

Web: www.bookleafpub.com

E-mail: info@bookleafpub.com

ISBN: 9789357747875

First edition 2023

To my amazing daughter, Alyla. To my devoted and supportive husband, William. Lastly, to my mother, Diane. Your selflessness has made me who I am today. You are forever missed.

ACKNOWLEDGEMENT

William H. M. Redmond
• I could not have undertaken this journey without you. You have always believed in me, even when I've doubted myself. You are the glue in our family. The best husband and father a woman could ask for. I love you so very much.

Alyla H. M. Redmond
• Words can not express my love for you. You inspire me every day to be a better person. Our lives were not complete until you came into this world. My smart, sassy, and beautiful daughter.

Lina DeMari Stacy
• I'm extremely grateful to you. A friend through the years. You have listened to my poetry for more than half our lives, and still appreciate it. You might be my biggest fan. Thank you for all your support and input. It is deeply treasured and valued. I would not have had the courage to pull this off without you.

Bre Murray-Begay

• I would like to express my deepest gratitude to you. We are like sisters, I'm not sure anyone knows me as well. We have bonded and endured so much together. I hope the future years are kinder to us, and that our friendship stands the test of time.

Jennifer M. Yule

• I would like to extend my sincere thanks to my sister. You are always a phone call away, helping me see things from a different perspective. Everyone needs someone like you in their lives. I am lucky to have you as a sister.

BookLeaf

• I had the pleasure of working with your publishing company. I wanted to thank you for this opportunity and experience.

Photographer

• Lastly, I'd like to acknowledge Inner Grace Photography. My photographer took amazing photos and was a genuinely nice person. Thank you. My book wouldn't be complete without your efforts.

https://www.facebook.com/InnerGracePhotogra
phy?mibextid=ZbWKwL

PREFACE

In writing this poetry book, I purged my soul. Putting into writing things that have been eating away at me for years and letting them go. It was a struggle at times. It's very vulnerable putting down your inner thoughts.

I published these poems for two purposes. One, to free myself. Is there still turmoil? Yes! But softer now. Two, in hopes others would identify with my words and feel their own experiences come to life. Letting my vulnerability spark your own.

I don't want to explain my poetry. They all have particular meaning to me. However, once they are written, they have the power to be your stories, too. I hope you find inner emotions and feelings with the words and maybe even some reconciliation with yourself.

Smoke Signals

There are moments forgotten. Sometimes they sneak in.
Like a tidal wave of capsaicin. Burning deep, rouge inflamed skin.
The memories of ghosts of the past. Taking hold.
A gullet filled with glass. Invisible tears burn my face as they fall.
I've lost all feeling. Everything and nothing at all.
Apathetic intensity my flesh struggles to contain.
No composure maintained. Like a spiky flashback.
Losing all control.
It crawled out from under a rock. It fell out of my soul.
I cannot swallow. Embers in my throat.
How can I feel so hollow? Gagging on ash.
Drowning in pools of water passed.
Lost in the depths of that one scene.
Playing on a loop. A terrible dream.
That one place. Subside now, you've filled every space. I can't say how.
There are moments best left forgotten.
But sometimes they sneak in.
Like a whirlwind of fire sending smoke signals.
From within.

Beyond Grief

Whispers of weakness, cluttered soul.
Vague accusations of guilt.
Shame for things beyond control.
Remorse and anguish felt.
Bad timing, my sentence.
Belief in others the crime.
Screams of culpability, muddled voice.
The weakness, there wasn't time.
Suffering forever with guilt.
Ticking of a clock.
But time has stopped.
Compunction sucks up the air.
Imprisoned in my regret.
Shackled to this shame.
Locked away in utter misery.
Shattered voice.
Mutters of accountability, crippled soul.
Perpetually burdened.
For things beyond control.

Ode To Alyla

Dear Moon
I've watched you grow from my belly
I love you
Deep in my soul
Dear Moon
You are perfect
No matter who you are
You shine bright forever
Shine brighter than the stars
I'll try to be your sun
Forever nurturing your light
Dear orb of the night
Please know I am truly yours
Through every fight
Through every meteor shower
I won't leave your sight
Dear Moon
My little lunar muse
You'll forever be teaching me
Forgive me if I don't get it quite right
Try as I might
Just know I am by your side
Forever your mother
You'll forever be my pride

Haunted

Haunting these walls. Haunting this room.
Ghosts of the past. A heart filled with gloom.
Never really seen. But whispers always felt.
Tender in a timid flesh. You feel her as a welt.
Goosebumps on the body. A plague on your
mind.
Do you feel her whisper? A numbing coolness
that's unkind.
Do you hear her wails? It sounds like a shrieking
wind.
An eerie air is her tell. I know you feel this
within.
A tumultuous storm. A haunting gloom.
She's always here, trapped in this room.

Mercy For A Hardened Heart

I am not angry
Part of me understands
It must be so hard to be a man
I know I'm not worthless
Many days I thought that was true
It's hard to be human
It was hard being you
I am not resentful
I see a clearer picture now
You wanted to love me
You just didn't know how
I carried this burden inside
For far too long
You can now forgive yourself
I have moved on
I see you differently now
All the sadness inside
The person you could have been
Had you been taught that feelings don't have to
hide
I am hopeful now
Something you never had
A love without conditions
Freedom to be sad
Freedom to convey love

And to take it in
A love you always had
It was always within

It must be so hard to be a man

Falling Into The Cracks

I wish I knew where I started. This strange journey. Brisk words constantly stinging my cheeks as I climb these sharp ridges. I am alone. Alone from myself.

Lost in an abyss of silence. My own thoughts cling like shrink wrap. Engulfing my every facility. Trapped in this arctic mirror. The storm rages in this nightmare of my own creation. When was I lost?

There is no peace here. Whistling gusts of glass hit my face. I do not care. It's been a while, but I'd know this place anywhere. Purgatory. Hell. I lost myself here. Where did I start?

Time nonexistent. A place where I was myself. Before I forgot. A window, before the walls slammed down. In this deserted, endless, empty box. But when did the clock stop?

Fragments of mimicked identities glistening between the cracks. I will forever be falling into the cracks. Forever in this misery of forgetting how to be myself. When did it get so dark?

Derailed, The Game Of Dismay

Running through life like a freight train
Playing roulette with choices
Making bets on your chances of survival
A life in dismay
Frantic with anxious anticipation
Unable to settle your soul
Staying still is not an option
Blackjack, the house always wins
Oh, look, you're back where you started
Destructive behavior again
Caught up in a frantic panic, unstable
Unable to gain back control
You'll never win
If only you keep moving
One foot in front of the next
Maybe you'll beat this addiction
Maybe you'll pass this test
All the cards are on the table
But the house always wins
A life in dismay
What are the chances of surviving,
When life goes so fast
What are the chances of surviving,
When the train won't stay on the tracks

Gehenna

All these memories faded, dwindling, like an
hourglass lost in time.
There are these moments I vaguely remember.
But I feel them in the dark.
Echos beating.
Somewhere out of reach.
Behind a wall.
I can feel them bleeding.
Telling me something is broken.
What it is, I can't recall.

A moment lost in time.
They sound so faded; I can't hear them at all.
Memories of something behind a downpour.
Sheets of rain falls.
Thunder all-encompassing, no lightning to guide
the way.
An eerie feeling looming.
These memories, they won't stay.

Behind these heavy curtains.
No visibility inside this dense fog.
The veil of amnesia has left me no choice, but to
navigate the darkness.
Searching for my voice.

The remembrance of stories somewhere hidden
deep.
A cave of time that's sinking.
Pulling me in.
I slowly seep.

The rain is deafening.
The thunder cracks against these dark walls.
It seems closer every inch I sink.
I still see nothing at all.
All these memories foreboding of a moment lost
in time.
Just outside my reach.
Someplace in my mind.

The Destroyer

Little voice, little voice
Let me in
I will control you and dampen your soul again

Little cry, little cry
Let me lie
I will break you and you'll never understand why

Little scream, little scream
Let me out
I will belittle you and fill you with doubt

Little sob, little sob
Let me wipe your tears
I see all your weaknesses and prey on your fears

Little wail, little wail
Let me win
I will always be, your only friend

February Rain

February rain came

It poured against the window sills
Everything stood still

It was the end of winter

But not yet spring
The day I heard the phone ring

A month like any other
But that day unlike the rest

Rain beating down
Matching the pounding in my chest

February Frozen in time
Instilled forever in my mind

A day like any other
But unlike the rest

Game Of Oppression

Your words sting like poison,
Killing everything in the room.
Preying on the feeble.
Oh, you are so strong!
Always keeping us underfoot.
You were a giant.
We were so small.
Breaking backs with words,
To make you feel tall.
Oh, you were so feared.
You liked it that way.
Words like daggers,
Killing all dreams.
Tearing down any hope.
You had to control it all.
To the world you were grinning,
Always playing the part.
Behind closed door seething,
Planting manipulative seeds
And poisoning hearts

Fibromyalgia

Pain in my hands, pain down my spine
This ill body I call mine
I try to escape it
Try to push through
But it's always there to remind me
Of the little I can do
Must this last forever
Must this be my fate
Must I always be in this tortured state
Pain in my stomach
Pain in my neck
Doomed to put a smile on
Even with this lousy deck
The cards that unfolded
Were not very kind
But I wake each day determined to find
A way to make it through this
A way to push past
A way to not let this misery become too vast
Pain that lasts forever
Pain that dulls my mind
Living in my dreams
The only escape I find
But I will make it through this
But I will make the good days count

But I won't let it destroy my soul
Or the little joys I've found

Diane

A piece of me is gone forever
It died with you
They said I'd feel better by now
But the pain keeps seeping through
Time doesn't heal this
It still hurts the same
It comes in like a flood
Especially when I hear your name
They tell me their stories
Acting like it's the same
Until you lose a mother
You won't know my pain
A pain that lasts forever
It doesn't get better with time
A mother is a permanent home
And I lost mine
They say it gets easier
Still waiting for that day
But if it means I forget you
I wish it away
I hope to keep you in me
Even if it hurts this bad
Because forgetting is worse
Then all this pain I have
I hope I always reach to call you

Even though it stings
I hope to always see you
In the littlest things
A mother's love is forever
I finally know what that means
A soul that is tethered
Without strings
I refuse to forget you
Refuse to move on
I will always love you
You were my Mom

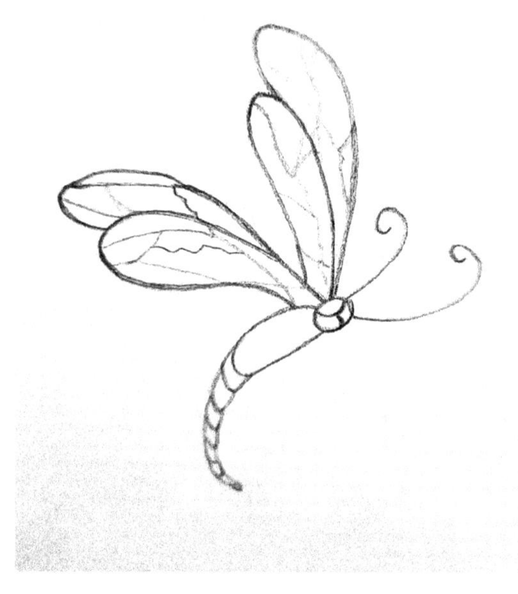

Lucid

Gentle sleep lay me down,
Taking me over.

Rhythmic waves of ease I lay,
Settling in, until the world fades away.

Tantalizing world's come alive.
Universe of my own creation,
I've found inside.

Sagas of importance where I am the player.
Oh, sweet dreams, take me over.

This world is vibrant.
Full of possibility and awe.

A place I've mastered.
Gentle lullaby, take me, please,
To worlds unknown.

Let me stay here a while longer.
Basking beneath these trees.
Don't wake me just yet.
Let me live this fantasy.

A few moments longer.

Dear Friend

Dear friend, you are grieving
Wish you didn't have to bear this loss
Dear friend, it's okay you aren't weeping
None of us face this journey the same way
Loss is so heavy
A different person you become
I know you say you weren't ready
But I have a feeling, that day would never have
come
There's never a good time to lose someone
Dear friend, I see the power in you
Not to forget,
But to live on
Dear friend, you did so much living
But none of it was for yourself
You must stay strong
Now you'll feel her in your choices
All she wants is happiness for you
So dear friend, do your grieving
Please do it how you need to do
But do as she wishes
And find happiness
It's all she ever wanted for you

Ineffable Night Sky

Stars raining from the sky
Cascading down like waterfalls
The sky is falling
Flooding the night with glowing embers
Fires burst from the atmosphere
Exploding like fireworks
Sparks sizzling down to the earth
The sky is falling
Can we watch it fall together?
Hold my hand as the world ends
The earth rumbles beneath us
Flowers of fire flicker for us
And us alone

Yesterday Brought Me Here

Looking at yesterday
I see sadness and loss
But today I have hope
Look at all the mountains I've crossed

Yesterday's sorrows all have their place
They grew us strong
We Must leave them behind
We Must move on

We can write them down
We mustn't forget
But to dwell in the past
It's a fool's regret

Living on despite them
Because yesterday is gone
But today and tomorrow
Has yet to be sung

Yesterday brought me here
Not what I lack
Made me who I am
It won't hold me back

Bittersweet Duality

Once, there was a girl named Happy
She was jovial from head to toe
Full of wonder and excitement
There was so much she didn't know
She skipped around each day with curiosity
Feeling that the world was hers
She did all things at full velocity
Sweetness, with a twirl

Once, there was a girl named Misery
She was sullen from head to toe
Full of skepticism and apathy
There was so much she didn't know
She shuffled her feet with pessimism
Feeling the world had lost its mind
She did all things with empathy
While morose, she was still kind

Once, there was a girl named Bittersweet
She was mixed up from head to toe
Filled with wonder and apathy
There was so much she didn't know
She skipped around each day with pessimism
Feeling she could own the madness, given some time

She did all things with empathy
While ambivalent, she was not unkind
She did all things at full velocity
Sweetness, with a twirl
Bittersweet her name, but she was both girls

Home

My house is sturdy
A place I call home
A palace we built
Out of brick and stone

My house is plenty
Sitting on my porch
Birds singing to each other
A beautiful chorus

My home is blissful
All the sounds
Trees that dance in the gentle wind
Oh what peace I have found

Our house is inviting
Filled with kindness to others
Understanding and goodness
Cherishing one another

My home is filled with love
No hesitation to be yourself
Sheer devotion to each other
Above all else

Reminders

Crawling through life.
These thoughts lay heavy on me.
Monoliths chained to my back.
I keep crawling.
Trying to get past them, but just dragging them
along.
Every trauma has its weight.
It never leaves you.
For decades I was a prisoner of this burden.
It was not mine to carry.
Trying so hard to turn these boulders into
pebbles.
Slowly chipping them away.
I've found a way.
I can move forward now.
I can stand.
These stones and chunks are still heavy.
No longer crippled by mass and damage.
Fashioning reminders of who I want to be out of
pebbles.
Every tribulation has its weight to carry.
It will pin you down, like a headstone.
But we have the strength to erode them.
Take away their power.
Condense them into reminders.

little reminders of where we came from,
And where we don't belong.
Turning standing stones into gravel.
We can stand,
To move on.
No more a prisoner
Full of reminders.
Rocks are formidable.
But we can be stronger.
With tenacity we can be indestructible.
Turning monoliths into sand.
I must believe we can.

She Rides The Wind

She rides the wind. A blossom in the storm.
Stardust that's fizzling down. Indestructible.

Always quick to mend. Completely adaptable.
A force to be reckoned with. A cobra with
venomous love.
Too stubborn to fail.

Trauma is her backbone. You can see it down
her spine. But it will never tear her down. No,
she will always be fine.

Poison oozing through her veins. Lace flowing
down her skin.
Can't let you fall.
knowing the pain.
She has felt it all.

Tragically empathetic.
Feeling all the world's woes.

Suck it in and siphon out your pain. Take it all
away.
But that isn't possible.
Just torture instead.

A fragile calla lily. Rebirth after the rain.
Delicate and unbreakable.

Strength evolved from rotting roots. Tremendous
loss and still boasting with guts. She can't let
them win.

She rides the wind.

www.ingramcontent.com/pod-product-compliance
Lightning Source LLC
La Vergne TN
LVHW010934200726
843509LV00013B/2217